How To Teach Social Skills

Marion V. Panyan

How To Manage Behavior Series

R. Vance Hall
and
Marilyn L. Hall
Series Editors

8700 Shoal Creek Boulevard
Austin, Texas 78757-6897

8700 Shoal Creek Boulevard
Austin, Texas 78757-6897

Library of Congress Cataloging-in-Publication Data

Panyan, Marion V.
How to teach social skills / Marion V. Panyan.
p. cm.—(How to manage behavior series)
Includes bibliographical references.
ISBN 0-89079-761-7 (alk. paper)
1. Social skills—Study and teaching. 2. Social skills in children—Study and teaching. I. Title. II. Series.
HQ783.P295 1998
302'.14'071—dc21 97-43061
CIP

This book is designed in Palatino and Frutiger.

Production Director: Alan Grimes
Production Coordinator: Karen Swain
Managing Editor: Chris Olson
Art Director: Thomas Barkley
Designer: Lee Anne Landry
Staff Copyeditor: Suzi Hunn
Reprints Buyer: Alicia Woods
Preproduction Coordinator: Chris Anne Worsham
Project Editor: Debra Berman
Production Assistant: Dolly Fisk Jackson
Publishing Assistant: John Means Cooper

Printed in the United States of America

1 2 3 4 5 6 7 8 9 10 02 01 00 99 98

Contents

Preface to Series

The first edition of the *How To Manage Behavior Series* was launched some 15 years ago in response to a perceived need for teaching aids that could be used by therapists and trainers. The widespread demand for the series has demonstrated the need by therapists and trainers for nontechnical materials for training and treatment aids for parents, teachers, and students. Publication of this revised series includes many updated titles of the original series. In addition, several new titles have been added, largely in response to therapists and trainers who have used the series. A few titles of the original series that proved to be in less demand have been replaced. We hope the new titles will increase the usefulness of the series.

The editors are indebted to Steven Mathews, Vice President of PRO-ED, who was instrumental in the production of the revised series, as was Robert K. Hoyt, Jr. of H & H Enterprises in producing the original version.

These books are designed to teach practitioners, including parents, specific behavioral procedures to use in managing the behaviors of children, students, and other persons whose behavior may be creating disruption or interference at home, at school, or on the job. The books are nontechnical, step-by-step instructional manuals that define the procedure, provide numerous examples, and allow the reader to make oral or written responses.

The exercises in these books are designed to be used under the direction of someone (usually a professional) with a background in the behavioral principles and procedures on which the techniques are based.

The booklets in the series are similar in format but are flexible enough to be adapted to a number of different teaching situations and training environments.

R. Vance Hall, PhD, is Senior Scientist Emeritus of The Bureau of Child Research and Professor Emeritus of Human Development and Family Life and Special Education at the University of Kansas. He was a pioneer in carrying out behavioral research in classrooms and in homes. Marilyn L. Hall, EdD, taught and carried out research in regular and special public school classrooms. While at the University of Kansas, she developed programs for training parents to use systematic behavior change procedures and was a successful behavior therapist specializing in child management and marriage relationships.

As always, we invite your comments, suggestions, and questions. We are always happy to hear of your successes in changing your own behaviors and the behaviors of other persons to make your lives more pleasant, productive, and purposeful.

R. Vance Hall &
Marilyn L. Hall,
Series Editors

How To Manage Behavior Series

How To Maintain Behavior

How To Motivate Others Through Feedback

How To Negotiate a Behavioral Contract

How To Select Reinforcers

How To Teach Social Skills

How To Teach Through Modeling and Imitation

How To Use Group Contingencies

How To Use Planned Ignoring

How To Use Prompts To Initiate Behavior

How To Use Response Cost

How To Use Systematic Attention and Approval

How To Use Time-Out

Introduction

Strong interpersonal relationships characterize a successful school and define what it means to be a successful family or community. Traditionally schools have focused on academic skills and not intentionally taught social skills; however, the youth of today are too important, their families and communities are too important, to leave social skills training to chance. Proven social skills curricula and strategies are abundant; they simply need to be adopted.

Therefore, the purpose of this manual is to introduce successful social skills training methods and programs so that readers may improve their teaching, counseling, mentoring, and parenting skills. Such improvements may result in individuals having more socially appropriate skills today, as well as passing positive social skills on to the next generation.

How To Teach Social Skills is dedicated to my closest circle of friends—my parents, Margaret and Gerald Veeneman; my husband, Steve; and our son, Eric.

Rationale

Several trends in society and schools signal a need for social skills training. First, schools are called upon to provide more comprehensive services than ever before in addition to the traditional teaching–learning activities.

Second, more and more adults are adopting teaching roles as parent tutor, big brother or sister, or business mentor for a school-to-work program. People are recognizing and realizing the power of one-on-one relationships for the individual, especially during challenging times or transitional years.

Third, psychologists have given renewed attention to the importance of social skills. In his treatise on multiple intelligences, Gardner (1983) included intrapersonal and interpersonal areas as two of the intelligences. Schools based on this model recognize the priority of these skills in the design and implementation of new curricula (Boggeman, Hoerr, & Wallach, 1996). Goleman (1995) articulated the critical nature of everyday social interactions and the contributions of early emotional learnings to lifelong habits in his text, *Emotional Intelligence.*

Marion V. Panyan, PhD, is Professor and Department Chair, Department of Special Education, Counseling, and Rehabilitation at Drake University, Des Moines, IA. She has developed graduate programs for teachers serving students with special needs in collaborative ways at all levels both at Drake and Johns Hopkins University. Her current research examines instructional practices to advance each child's multiple intelligences.

Social skills training has always been justified in terms of preventing future problems and contributing to well-adjusted adolescents and adults. With the added complexities and stressors of everyday life in the new millennium, now more than ever, teaching needs to be grounded in thoughtful and respectful ways of relating to others.

This manual offers some suggestions in this direction. Although it is brief, it includes numerous in-depth leads for serious readers to pursue as they teach social skills.

Definition

Ask 10 different professionals to define social skills and you will get 10 different answers. The common elements that appear in many definitions were captured by Gresham (1986), who defined social skills as "those behaviors which, within a given situation, predict important social outcomes" (p. 5). This definition acknowledges the role of behavior, the context, and the outcomes. First and foremost, social skills are behaviors. Asking for help, introducing oneself, taking turns talking, and following rules are a few specific social skills. Although there are both cognitive and emotional levels of behaviors, that discussion is beyond the scope of this book. By *context,* I mean the conditions present when the social skill occurs. The context (e.g., a library) may suggest that talking in a quiet voice to ask a question is acceptable whereas a different context (e.g., a soccer game) may suggest that loud cheering is acceptable. By outcomes, I mean the reactions of peers and adults to the social skill.

Underlying Understandings

1. Social skills are *learned* skills, which can be positive or negative.
2. Social skills are as important as academic skills for success in life.
3. Social skill training is for all individuals, not only for those with major deficits or excesses.
4. Social skill instruction is an ongoing process, infused throughout the day, particularly *when* the behavior occurs.
5. Social skills can be systematically taught but are not easily generalized.
6. Social skills should be taught to young children to enhance their social–emotional development and as an inoculation against future difficulties.

Give an example of a situation where a social skill or lack of one has impacted a person's career, positively or negatively.

Practices Derived from the Initial Understandings

▶ **Step 1: Name the skill.**

Over the years educators have found it useful to focus on the action of the individual rather than an attribute of the individual in naming the skill. For example, describing a high school student as apathetic or a preschooler as withdrawn conjures up many images. To be more precise, one could say that the high school student doesn't participate in group discussions during English class or that a preschooler doesn't interact with his or her peers. Many times the behaviors that lead to or interfere with learning or social interactions are communicated in vague terms that are difficult to measure. For example, one cannot measure good sportsmanship, but one can measure the number of times a member of one team congratulates or shakes hands with members of the opposing team. By naming social behaviors in ways that can be measured, one can track improvements. Precisely defining a behavior helps to (a) clarify the present behavior, (b) set a goal based on this behavior, and (c) measure progress toward that goal.

Read each of the following pairs of phrases describing social skills. Check the one that names the behavior in specific terms.

1. ☐ Holds hands in circle games
   ☐ Plays cooperatively
2. ☐ Appreciates others and tries to make them feel welcome
   ☐ Asks a new student to join his or her group

(*continues*)

3. ☐ Is a very friendly and outgoing person
   ☐ Makes eye contact with another and says, "Good morning"
4. ☐ Shows examples of merchandise to customer
   ☐ Responds to customer's needs
5. ☐ Makes insensitive and tactless remarks
   ☐ Says, "That's a poor idea"
6. ☐ Acts like a bully, confronts and intimidates others
   ☐ Stands face to face with a person and says, "Do this or else"

Translate the following attributes sometimes ascribed to others into specific social behaviors. Write your action verbs next to the attribute.

Attribute	Action
jovial	______________________
aggressive	______________________
rude	______________________
sensitive	______________________
withdrawn	______________________

Actions associated with a person who is jovial might be "smiles," "laughs," and "tells jokes." Some actions that may be associated with aggressive behavior would be "hitting," "kicking," and "breaking windows." Naming the behavior or behaviors that constitute aggression for the individual is the first step in initiating a plan for change.

Basically, this plan is aimed to help the individual develop positive skills (e.g., complimenting a peer, rearranging desks for group study) and to reduce the frequency of other skills (e.g., hitting a classmate or neighbor, making critical remarks toward another person).

▶ Step 2: Record and measure the social skills.

Measurement procedures are used to determine the level of behavior before intervention and how well the behavior responds to intervention. Because social skills are defined by their impact on others, it is logical that the perceptions of others constitute an important part of the measurement process. Three useful approaches for measuring social skills are (a) adult and peer ratings, (b) direct observation, and (c) functional assessment.

Adult and Peer Ratings

The *Social Skills Rating System* (SSRS) (Gresham & Elliott, 1990) permits teachers, peers, or parents to rate the student on two key dimensions of social skills: frequency and importance. The results of this system show the ratings for each student on each skill, but also each student's ratings in relation to the class as a whole. Similar scales include the *Social Behavior Assessment* (Stephens, 1979) and the *Scale of Social Competence* (Walker & McConnell, 1988). In each instance a companion volume specifying social skills intervention tactics is provided.

Explain why adult ratings are important in measuring social skills.

____

____

____

____

Direct Observation

Using direct observation and careful recording, one can capture the behavior as it happens or soon after. A recorder notes the presence or frequency of a social skill during a preset time period. The presence of initiations for young children at play during 15-second intervals was noted by Collins, Ault, Hemmeter, and Doyle (1996). Their scoring system also included the names of the children toward whom the child made initiations. The frequency of a social behavior was noted in a study where an eighth-grade student counted the number of talk-outs he made (Broden, Hall, & Mitts, 1971).

Another example of direct observation is a parent who set her microwave timer at varying intervals averaging 30 seconds. When the timer sounded, she noted whether her 7-year-old daughter was sharing materials in an art project with her 5-year-old brother. The mother recorded this information 10 times a day for 3 days. Because her daughter's teacher had complained that the child was possessive and rarely offered to share her belongings, the parent's record would support or refute this concern at home. If it was a problem in the home, steps could be taken to correct it.

The frequency of a social behavior is noted by counting and recording the behavior each time it occurs within a time period (e.g., day, class, recess).

Sometimes social behaviors leave behind evidence of their action on the environment. Graffiti on school walls, broken windows, torn textbooks, and toys left in the middle of the room all leave permanent products. The number of torn pages in textbooks, for example, can represent the level and severity of behavior before intervention if the adult has observed the student engaging in the behavior. The same products (i.e., torn pages) could be used during or after intervention to see if the treatment worked. Although some products reflect the level of behavior, they do not always provide as precise a record as other methods. One difficulty is that one may not be sure who produced the effect (e.g., graffiti). It may have been one child or several students who wrote on the walls.

Hall and Van Houten (1977) described a variety of options to easily and reliably record behaviors in natural settings. Their recommendations, data forms, and charts are useful in measuring and monitoring social skills.

A variation of standard recording systems for one individual is the response discrepancy evaluation method (Rhode, Jenson, & Reavis, 1992). With this method, the target student is observed along with a randomly selected same-sex peer. For example, the target student's behavior of completing assigned work is recorded during the first 10-second interval. A dot is placed in the interval if he is completing his work and an off-task code if he is not. One peer is also observed, whose behavior is recorded during the same interval. Next, the observer records the behavior of the target student and a different peer. This pattern continues for 15 minutes. Thus, the target student's behavior and that of one of his peers are being recorded every 10 seconds.

The purpose of this recording method is to gauge the level of a specific student's social skill in relation to the class as a whole. The percentage of intervals of completing assignments might be 42% for the target student and 89% for his peers, thus showing a wide discrepancy and need for intervention. When these results are shared with the target student, he might become more aware of group norms in an objective fashion. The literature shows that awareness of group norms is a major dimension of social competence (Putallaz & Gottman, 1982).

See Appendixes A and B for sample recording forms for social behaviors. Appendix A illustrates a form to use for a behavior where you want to note the presence or absence of a behavior at a certain time. These times can be cued by a wall clock, a watch alarm, a microwave timer, or a vibrating pager. Appendix B shows a form for use in instances where you want to count the number of times a behavior occurred.

Select a specific social behavior of someone that is of concern to you and describe one direct observational method to record it.

____

____

____

Functional Assessment

Another type of measurement provides clues as to what or who is maintaining the behavior. The idea is that people behave in antisocial ways because they get something out of it or, more technically speaking, it serves a function. For example, Mario throws tantrums in his primary multi-age classroom. The teacher could have a recorder count the number of tantrums or time the length of each tantrum. This would help to describe the behavior, but not necessarily provide a clue to design an appropriate intervention. By gathering some additional information, such as what happened right before the tantrum and what happened after it, the teacher can learn more about the function(s) the tantrums serve.

For example, the teacher might learn that the tantrums are associated with math and no other academic period. She might learn that the typical response to the tantrums is that she and the student's peers stop their work and immediately attend to Mario when he tantrums. These two facts alone give direction to the treatment. It appears that Mario might be engaging in tantrums to escape from unpleasant or difficult work and / or to receive attention from his teachers and peers. The teacher would then examine the nature of the math curriculum. Perhaps a hands-on approach could be used to help Mario understand the concepts. If Mario was not injuring himself or others, perhaps his tantrums could be ignored. If Mario's tantrums decrease once these two changes are made, then the analysis was correct. If his tantrums continue, then the teacher needs to examine other functions they may be serving for Mario, such as sensory feedback.

In summary, a functional assessment requires more data to make decisions regarding the function that a behavior serves for an individual. However, once this function has been identified, a more appropriate and individualized treatment can be initiated. A sample functional assessment form is shown in Appendix C. For more information on how to conduct a functional assessment, see *Functional Analysis of Problem Behavior: A Practical Assessment Guide* (O'Neill, Horner, Albin, Storey, & Sprague, 1990).

▶ Step 3: Set goals.

Once the skill has been named, the next step is to set the goal with the individual. Goal setting itself can change behavior and, by involving the person concerned, send a message that what he or she thinks matters.

The following are important guidelines in setting a goal:

1. Include the conditions and criterion in the goal. Describe the conditions that surround the social skill (e.g., "*Before using a peer's belongings,* the student will use 'please' to introduce the specific request.") Describe the criterion by stating how well or how often the skill is to be demonstrated (e.g., "*Each time* the student uses a peer's belongings, he will preface the specific request with 'please'").

2. Make sure the person understands what behavior is expected of him or her. Often when I visit classrooms, I ask students to explain their goal for the day, week, or month. This tells me whether the student knows what is expected of him or her. If the student does not understand, then the expectations can be clarified. For example, Polaroid pictures depicting acceptable social skills can be used as reminders of the goal behavior.

3. Make sure the student is aware of his or her behavior. Sometimes individuals with long histories of a behavior are not aware of how often they actually engage in it. One way to determine if they are aware of the frequency of the behavior is to let them count it for a period of time while you count the same behavior. Studies have shown that self-recording sometimes is sufficient to change a behavior (Broden, Hall, & Mitts, 1971).

4. Select a behavior that can be mastered. As an example, imagine you are teaching a high school student the skills involved in interviewing. You might first teach a series of behaviors to enter the office, greet the interviewer, and introduce oneself. These behaviors could be videotaped in a role-play situation. After the student has mastered these skills, then elements of the interview conversation could be taught, followed by the closing statements and departure skills.

5. Gather information on community, class, or work norms. Social norms vary considerably, and therefore a goal is culturally bound. What is acceptable in one group might be disdained in a different group. Therefore, systems such as the response discrepancy evaluation method described earlier, which take into account the prevailing norms, should be considered.

6. Seek input from significant others who frequently interact with the individual. Listening to others makes it more certain that the student will come into contact with natural communities of reinforcement to maintain the social skill.

List the numbers of the goal-setting recommendations that were followed in this scenario on the line after the example:

> The goal for a seventh-grade student who was habitually tardy for class was to arrive on time. This goal is in keeping with class norms and later job expectations. The teacher whose class the student attended was consulted so that she might reinforce his punctual behavior.
>
> ______________________________

Set a goal that includes the condition and criterion for the social skill you identified earlier as of concern to you.

Condition: ______________________________

Goal (includes original behavior you identified): ______________________________

Criterion: ______________________________

▶ Step 4: Teach social skills.

Many curricula are available as guides to teach social skills (e.g., Elliott & Gresham, 1991; McGinnis & Goldstein, 1984, 1990; Walker et al., 1983; Walker, Todis, Holmes, & Horton, 1988). These curricula effectively describe a range of challenging behaviors and ways to systematically teach alternate behaviors. Many of the behaviors reflect adult relations, peer relations, school rules, and classroom behaviors. A process for evaluating and selecting social skills curricula has been designed by Carter and Sugai (1989) and Sugai and Fuller (1991). Regardless of the curriculum chosen, it is important that the school faculty agree on the curriculum and weave it into their schedule on a regular basis.

Model Appropriate Social Skills

A high school student with a mental disability who had been served in special education classrooms all his life typically hugged anyone and everyone, stranger or friend. When he moved to an inclusive biology class, he soon found that other young men were quickly turned off by hugs. The students taught him a high-five gesture as an alternate way to say hello. He watched his peers interact and modeled their responses.

A news story reported on a 2-year-old boy who dialed 911 when his mom needed help. He learned this skill by watching Big Bird on Sesame Street dial that number in an emergency.

Unfortunately modeling alone does not always have an impact. People often need to be provided with reinforcement for attending to a model and for performing social behaviors that have been modeled. Several models appear to generate better results than relying on a single model. Films, videotapes, computer programs, live demonstrations, and stories can all provide relevant examples. Some of these methods portray nuances of nonverbal skills that are central to social skill success (Duke, Nowicki, & Martin, 1996).

Analyze and Arrange the Environment To Prompt Social Skills

A group of first and second graders are delving into modes of transportation as part of a group investigation. Several group members work together on an assignment that contributes to the completion of the project (e.g., obtain a book on trucks from the library, make a model plane from balsa wood, draw a picture of boats). Many cooperative formats encourage positive peer interactions, such as the jigsaw approach (Aronson & Patnoe, 1997), the cooperative lesson (Johnson, Johnson, & Holubec, 1994), and the student team learning model (Slavin, 1991).

Rehearse the Social Skill

Behavioral rehearsal provides an opportunity to perform the new social skill in a safe setting, much like a dress rehearsal for a play or a mock interview. People rehearsing the skill do not actually experience negative consequences (e.g., lose the job if they fail to provide appropriate answers). Rather, the trainer provides feedback as the students rehearse and hone their skills in role-play situations.

Reinforce the Social Skill

Working and playing well with others, volunteering to help peers, and receiving criticism well are all social behaviors worthy of reinforcement. Positive reinforcement is virtually anything you provide after a behavior that makes that behavior more likely to happen again. Smiles, praise, treats, music, and points toward a field trip or special outing, such as a baseball game or movie, are examples of reinforcement. Reinforcers should be given immediately and enthusiastically for behaviors that move the student toward his or her goal and withheld for behaviors that turn the student away from that goal. For example, Lori's goal was to wait in line for her turn to use the instruments in the music box. If Lori waited quietly for 2 minutes, she would be praised by the teacher. The teacher might say, "Lori, I see you are waiting your turn; you can pick out an instrument in just a few minutes." However, if Lori was complaining while waiting, she would be ignored, or if she was pushing, she would be told to go to the end of the line.

Providing positive reinforcement frequently and consistently can help teach the student to learn a new social skill or to maintain one he or she has already learned. See another book in this series (i.e., *How To Use Systematic Attention and Approval,* Hall, & Hall, 1998a) for a more complete discussion of reinforcing consequences.

Describe how you might prompt or reinforce the social skill you have identified as your goal. Be sure to address these concerns:

1. Where might an appropriate model of the social skill be found? ________

   ____

2. How will you arrange the setting to prompt the response? ____________

   ____

3. What reinforcers will you use when the social skill occurs? ____________

   ____

   ____

Capitalize on the Teachable Moment

One of the best times to teach social skills is exactly when a misbehavior occurs. Astute adults can turn such occasions into a corrective teaching interaction. As first documented in *The Teaching–Family Handbook* (Phillips, Phillips, Fixsen, & Wolf, 1974), there are nine components of a teaching interaction: (1) express affection, (2) praise initially, (3) describe inappropriate behavior, (4) describe appropriate behavior, (5) offer a rationale, (6) request acknowledgment, (7) practice and feedback, (8) provide consequences, and (9) provide general praise. The following scenario from the manual *School Social Skills: A Teaching Approach to Schoolwide Discipline* (Wells, 1991) illustrates these steps.[1]

---

[1]From *School Social Skills: A Teaching Approach to Schoolwide Discipline* (pp. 66–67), by P. L. Wells, 1991, unpublished manuscript. Reprinted with permission of the author.

Skill: How To Greet Someone

As this scene begins, student and teacher are passing each other in the hallway. After the initial inappropriate greeting, the student responds appropriately by looking at the teacher and following all instructions.

TEACHER: (Looks at student, smiles) "Good morning (*Name*)."

STUDENT: (Looks away, mumbles) "Hi." (Continues walking)

TEACHER: "(*Name*), I need to see you for a moment, please."

[Corrective teaching begins here.]

Expression of Affection

TEACHER: (Smiles, looks at student, uses quiet voice tone)

Initial Praise

"(*Name*), thanks for coming here. It's good to see you at school today!

Description of Inappropriate Behavior

"(*Name*), when I greeted you just now, you returned my greeting, but looked down, mumbled 'Hi,' and hurried by.

Description of Appropriate Behavior

"Whenever you greet people, you need to look at them, smile, and then give a complete verbal greeting like, 'Good morning, (*Name*)!' using a pleasant voice tone.

Rationale

"A greeting like that will show others that you're friendly and happy to see them and may make them feel good too.

Request for Acknowledgment

"Do you see how greeting others can help you make friends?"

STUDENT: "Yes, I do."

TEACHER: "Good. What are the steps for greeting others?"

STUDENT: "You look at the person, smile, and give a verbal greeting using a pleasant voice tone."

Practice

TEACHER: "That's right. Let's practice that greeting. I'll stand here. I'd like you to back up a few feet, then come up to me once again. This time, remember those four steps we just talked about. Okay?"

STUDENT: "Okay."

(Student backs up, approaches teacher and greets appropriately)

"Good morning, (*Name*)!"

TEACHER: (Smiles, warm voice tone)

"Good morning, (*Name*)!"

Feedback

"Excellent practice! You looked at me, smiled, and said 'Good morning, (*Name*)' with a pleasant voice tone.

Consequence

"Because you initially had problems with your greeting, we're both late getting to class and you've also missed your journal writing. So, you'll need to take your journal home to make your entry before tomorrow. But, since you practiced greeting me so well and accepted my criticism, your tardy will be excused."

STUDENT: "Thanks!"

General Praise

TEACHER: "I'll write you an excuse . . . and you need to get to homeroom so you can hear announcements."

Role-Playing the Use of Corrective Teaching Interactions: Work with two other people (e.g., family member, instructor, coworker) to role-play the preceding example, taking the roles of teacher, student, and recorder. As the teacher and student read their parts from the script, the recorder checks off each component of the teaching interaction as it is completed.

(*continues*)

- ☐ Expression of affection
- ☐ Initial praise
- ☐ Description of inappropriate behavior
- ☐ Description of appropriate behavior
- ☐ Rationale
- ☐ Request for acknowledgment
- ☐ Practice
- ☐ Practice feedback
- ☐ Consequence
- ☐ General praise

After this role-play is concluded, set up your own teaching interaction role-play situation and adopt a different role from the one you had in the first role-play situation. The three of you can collaborate on the script prior to the role-play using the outline provided.

First, set up the scene. At the beginning of the scene, the student

____

The adult's reaction is ______________________________

The student's response is ____________________________

Second, give an example of each of the following teaching interaction components:

Expression of affection ______________________________

Initial praise ______________________________________

Description of inappropriate behavior __________________

____

Description of appropriate behavior ___________________

____

(*continues*)

Rationale ____

____

Request for acknowledgment ______________________________

____

____

Practice ____

____

____

____

____

Feedback ____

Consequence ____

____

____

____

____

General praise ____

Now that you have written the script, it is time to act out the parts and for the recorder to note whether each component is completed. Congratulations on designing and rehearsing your own role-play!

Carter and Sugai (1989) listed the advantages and disadvantages of instructional tactics for teaching social skills. They concluded that using several of these techniques in combination leads to better outcomes than using one by itself.

Give an example using two or more social skill teaching practices together to teach a second-grade student to welcome a new student to the class.

▶ Step 5: Reduce inappropriate social skills.

By prompting and reinforcing prosocial skills, negative behaviors are less likely to develop. Also, by being attuned to factors in the home, school, and community that could trigger negative behaviors, and by making minor adjustments, the behavior sometimes improves. Despite these approaches, however, sometimes negative behaviors prevail and it is difficult to teach a new skill because the child's negative social behavior interferes. Therefore, in these situations, the negative behavior must be addressed directly.

Differential Reinforcement of Incompatible Behaviors

The most positive approach for treating negative behaviors is to teach an acceptable behavior that cannot occur at the same time as the negative behavior. For example, Ethel, a fourth grader, slaps a peer on the playground. Ethel could be taught and reinforced for dribbling a ball, because it is difficult to dribble a basketball and slap someone at the same time. Technically, this procedure is called differential reinforcement of an incompatible behavior, or simply DRI.

Using the DRI method, write a positive behavior next to the negative behavior that it would replace.

Negative Behavior	Positive Behavior
Tapping a pencil loudly on the desk	______________________
	______________________
Losing one's temper in conflicts with peers	______________________
	______________________
Making negative self-statements	______________________
	______________________

Time-Out from Positive Reinforcement

Many procedures, such as time-out, overcorrection, or removal of points or privileges, have proved effective in reducing or eliminating negative behavior. Time-out refers to time away from sources of reinforcement. The individual is placed in an area for a brief period (i.e., 3 to 10 minutes) after he or she has misbehaved. It is critical that the time-out area be plain, and that the time-in area be full of interesting and reinforcing activities. The time-out area should be explained to the individual before he or she misbehaves. For example, the teacher might say, "Sylvia, if you hit Samantha today, you will go sit in the chair behind the divider. Then, if and when Sylvia hits Samantha, the teacher instructs her to go to the chair and tells her she can get up when the timer goes off. It is helpful to use a timer to signal the end of the time-out period because (a) you might forget when the time is up, and (b) the child doesn't try to negotiate the time by asking, "Can I leave now?" Time-out seems to work because (a) there is a clear and consistent consequence for misbehavior, (b) reinforcement is removed for misbehavior, and (c) their peers learn that such behavior is not acceptable. However, some individuals actually prefer time-out and the space it affords them. Continue to keep records during treatment to see whether the behavior is improving and whether time-out is having its intended effect. For further discussion on this topic, see *How To Use Time-Out* (Hall & Hall, 1998b).

Overcorrection

One form of overcorrection called *positive practice* has been used to practice the appropriate behavior right after the misbehavior has occurred. For example, if a student ran out of the room before the bell rang, he or she would have to sit down, and then walk to the line five times before leaving. Another form of overcorrection is called *restitution* because an individual is making amends for his or her actions. In one study (Azrin & Wesolowski, 1974) involving theft at school, the thief had to return the stolen item but also another item to the person who had been robbed. Overcorrection teaches appropriate skills (e.g., apologizing to someone you hurt), and the exaggerated practice can be effective in changing behaviors. Students who respond best to this approach are those who follow instructions. For a student who does not follow instructions, it is necessary to physically guide him or her through the motions. This guided practice may not be feasible under normal classroom conditions.

Response Cost

Students can also be penalized for negative behaviors by losing something. Drivers who are stopped for speeding forfeit some of their earnings. In other words, it costs them to respond (i.e., speed). In much the same way, students can learn that certain behaviors that interfere with learning will be penalized. For example, students may earn tokens for prosocial behaviors but lose them for behaviors such as disrupting the group or starting fights. The student hands over the prespecified amount (e.g., 20 tokens) after the antisocial behavior. Two cautions in using this procedure are that (a) you must make sure that the individual has sufficient tokens that there are some to remove, and (b) you must see that there are no additional outbursts or struggles involved when tokens are removed. It must be a matter-of-fact transaction. See *How To Use Response Cost* (Thibadeau, 1998) in this series for other considerations in adopting this procedure.

▶ **Step 6: Evaluate social skills.**

Once a new behavior has been acquired, you need to check it periodically to make sure it is still strong. Likewise, after reducing or eliminating a behavior, you need to monitor it. The main reason for evaluating your approach is to see if it continues to be helpful for your child, student, or employee.

Elliott and Gresham (1991) provided an excellent example of a social skills intervention progress monitoring record. The progress assessment notes whether a skill has stayed the same, improved, been mastered, and/or generalized. These determinations can be made from adults' notes, journals, interviews, videos, feedback from community members, or more formal direct observations.

One of the best ways to detect changes over time and monitor progress is to chart the behavior. A chart or graph provides a clear view of how the behavior responds to the intervention.

Without some type of evaluation, you have no way of telling if your intervention is successful. More important, you may not pursue a new approach as quickly as you should to reverse the cycle of inappropriate social skills.

Enter the relevant information next to name, setting, and behavior definition on the behavior chart. Plot three data points on the graph in Appendix D for the first 3 days or beginning level of the social skill you plan to teach. Connect the three points and answer the following questions:

1. Is the behavior in need of intervention? Yes ☐ No ☐
2. What is your goal based on these three data points? ____________________

____

____

Draw a vertical line from the top to the bottom of the graph after the third session and before the fourth session. Plot the data for 3 days after you have introduced your social skill intervention program.

1. Did the behavior stay the same, improve, or get worse? ______________
2. Consider what action you would take now to develop or continue progress toward your goal.

   Would you continue treatment in its present form? Yes ☐ No ☐

   Would you change treatment? Yes ☐ No ☐

   If yes, name the specific intervention plan you would try. ______________

   ____

   ____

   ____

   ____

▶ Step 7: Extend social skills.

Although this step appears in this list as the final one, these strategies need to be considered even as you select a skill or goal. Research shows that social skills do not automatically transfer to new people and places. However, there are ways to increase chances that the new skills will be seen across time, in the presence of different people, and in various settings. When this happens, we say the skill has generalized. We can teach generalization in the following ways.

1. Involve socially competent peers, who reinforce and model appropriate social skills, in the intervention. Although contact alone is not sufficient, through repeated positive interactions and the opportunities to pursue common interests, friendships can be developed and maintained. Mannix (1995) described ways to foster friendship skills for secondary students with special needs.
2. Train in more than one setting. If you restrict training to a single setting, often the behavior will be seen only in that setting. However, if you teach the social skill in several settings, the behavior is likely to transfer to even more settings.
3. Select target behaviors that are likely to become entrapped in the natural community of reinforcers. Teaching a child to compliment others or to invite a peer to share a toy are two behaviors that will bring about a positive response from others. This positive response in turn will bring about another instance of complimenting or sharing in similar circumstances. Alber and Heward (1996) offered other ways to garner (trap) students in a success circle with such activities as band, safety patrol, and cooking club. Here the students learn to cooperate, negotiate, and provide assistance while receiving positive feedback from peers and adults.
4. Intervene directly in the setting where the social skill needs to be exhibited. If the problem occurs on the playground, that is where it must be addressed. If it occurs in the cafeteria, provide treatment in that setting rather than in the classroom or counselor's office.
5. Coordinate your efforts with other adults. For example, you might provide social skills homework that gives students an opportunity to practice their newly learned skills at home or in the neighborhood. Other options are to design a behavioral contract or provide daily report cards on social behavior to students and their parents.
6. Teach and require a child to self-manage his or her behavior. Self-management components that apply to social skills are self-monitoring, self-recording, self-instruction, goal setting, and self-evaluation. Excellent self-recording ideas and forms for elementary-age children are provided in McGinnis and Goldstein's (1984) guide for teaching prosocial skills.
7. Use as many examples and models as possible, and teach the student to tell the difference between appropriate and inappropriate social skills by

observing others, viewing videotaped sequences, or labeling illustrations in a book. By using multiple examples, the child does not narrowly define the behavior. Mannix (1986) developed a workbook to be used in teaching social behaviors critical for group work, such as waiting for help and handling classroom frustrations. The student is asked to put a smiley face next to the illustration of the proper behavior (i.e., "read the directions again") and a face with a frown next to the inappropriate behavior (i.e., "yell until the teacher comes over to you").

Which way(s) to promote the extension of social skills beyond the training situation might be useful in the following scenario?

A 4-year-old girl is playing a game by herself on the computer. Her 6-year-old brother approaches her and wants time on the computer.

In what ways will you promote generalization of the social skill(s) you have chosen to teach to someone in your situation?

Conclusion

No set of skills is more crucial to one's life and relationships than social skills. This book has summarized the many ways that social skills can be taught. The good news is that anyone can teach social skills. They are taught when a neighbor, bus driver, or brother models courteous behaviors; when a principal, aunt, or coach praises a child for playing fairly; and when a group home counselor uses positive practice as a consequence for violating a rule. This book is brief and is meant to be augmented with the references and further reading.

Because of the reciprocal nature of social skills, their acquisition is as reinforcing for the teacher as for the one who is being taught. A continuing cycle is set in motion each time a child says "please" or "thank you." I say "thank you" for reading this text and responding during the exercises. Good luck to you as you put these ideas into practice. Seek others to assist you along the way, and share your successes with others.

Appendix A
Recording Form
for Presence of a Behavior

Name ______________________ Date ______________________

Observer ______________________ Setting ______________________

Time start ______________________ Time stop ______________________

Social behavior ____

Time Observed	Was the Behavior Present?	Comments
____________	Yes ☐ No ☐	______________________
____________	Yes ☐ No ☐	______________________
____________	Yes ☐ No ☐	______________________
____________	Yes ☐ No ☐	______________________
____________	Yes ☐ No ☐	______________________
____________	Yes ☐ No ☐	______________________
____________	Yes ☐ No ☐	______________________
____________	Yes ☐ No ☐	______________________
____________	Yes ☐ No ☐	______________________
____________	Yes ☐ No ☐	______________________
____________	Yes ☐ No ☐	______________________
____________	Yes ☐ No ☐	______________________

Percentage is computed as follows:

$$\frac{\text{Total number of ``Yes'' answers}}{\text{Total number of times observed}}$$

Appendix B
Recording Form
for Frequency of a Behavior

Name ______________________________ Date ______________________

Observer ___________________________ Setting ____________________

Time start __________________________ Time stop __________________

Social behavior ____

Number of Times	**Behavior Directed to** (name of person if applicable)

Appendix C
Functional Assessment Form

Name ______________________ Date ______________________

Observer ______________________ Setting ______________________

Time start ______________________ Time stop ______________________

Social behavior ____

Time	Activity	Triggering Event	Consequences	Comments

Appendix D
Sample Form for Charting Behavior

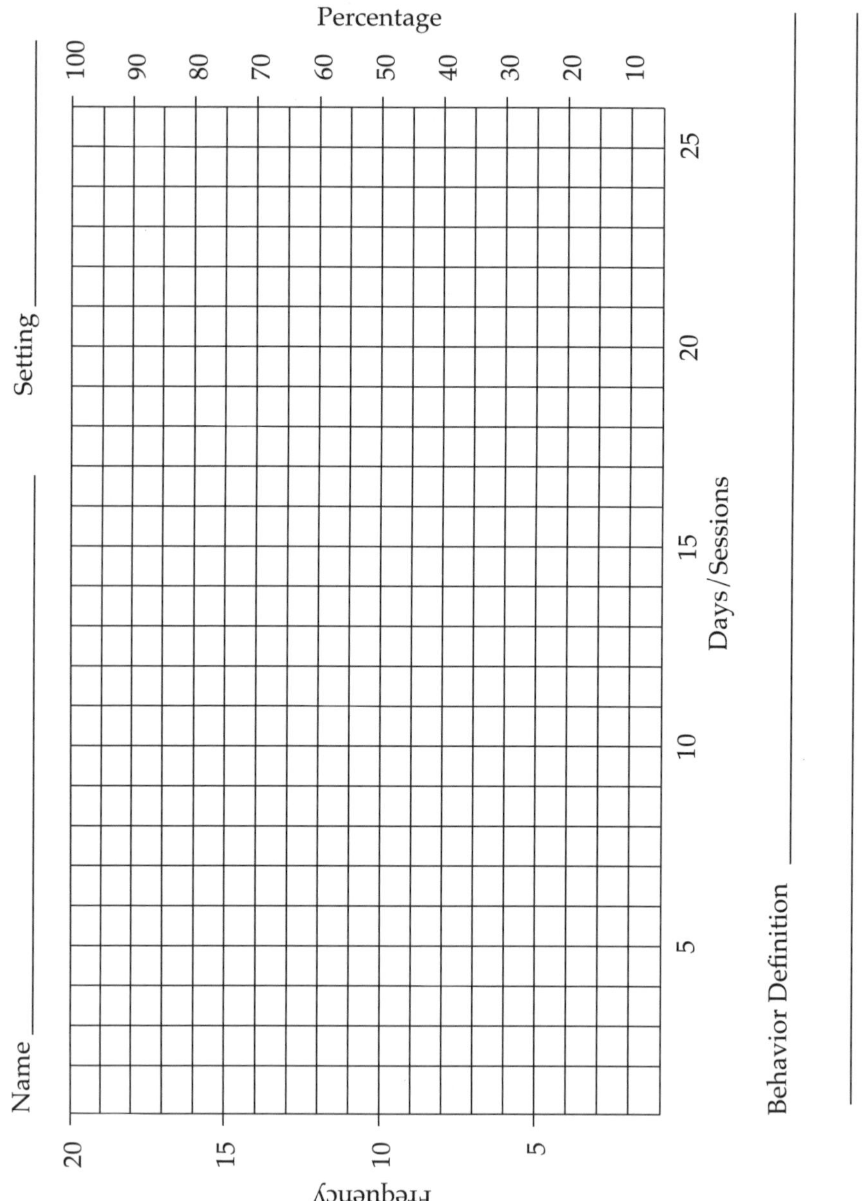

References and Further Reading

Alber, S. R., & Heward, W. L. (1996). "Gotcha!" Twenty-five behavior traps guaranteed to extend your students' academic and social skills. *Intervention in School and Clinic, 31*(5), 285–289.

Aronson, E., & Patnoe, S. (1997). *The jigsaw classroom* (2nd ed.). New York: Addison-Wesley.

Azrin, N. H., & Besalel, V. (1980) *How to use positive practice.* Austin, TX: PRO-ED.

Azrin, N. H., & Wesolowski, M. D. (1974). Theft reversal: An overcorrection procedure for eliminating stealing by retarded persons. *Journal of Applied Behavior Analysis, 7,* 577–581.

Boggeman, S., Hoerr, T., & Wallach, C. (1996). *Succeeding with multiple intelligences: Teaching through the personal intelligences.* St. Louis, MO: The New City School.

Broden, M., Hall, R. V., & Mitts, B. (1971). The effect of a self-recording on the classroom behavior of two eighth-grade students. *Journal of Applied Behavior Analysis, 4,* 191–199.

Brown, L. J., Black, D. D., & Downs, J. C. (1984). *School social skills manual.* New York: Slosson Educational.

Carter, J., & Sugai, G. (1989, Fall). Social skills curriculum analysis. *Teaching Exceptional Children,* pp. 36–39.

Cartledge, G., & Milburn, J. F. (1995). *Teaching social skills to children: Innovative approaches* (3rd ed.). Needham Heights, MA: Allyn & Bacon.

Collins, B. C., Ault, M. J., Hemmeter, M. L., & Doyle, P. M. (1996). Come play! Developing children's social skills in an inclusive preschool. *Teaching Exceptional Children, 29*(1), 16–21.

Duke, M. P., Nowicki, S., & Martin, E. A. (1996). *Teaching your child the language of social success.* Atlanta: Peachtree.

Elliott, S. N., & Gresham, F. M. (1991). *Social skills intervention guide: Practical strategies for social skills training.* Circle Pines, MN: American Guidance Service.

Gardner, H. (1983). *Frames of mind.* New York: Basic Books.

Goldstein, A. P., Sprafkin, R. P., Gershaw, M. J., & Klein, P. (1980). *Skillstreaming the adolescent: A structured learning approach to teaching prosocial skills.* Champaign, IL: Research Press.

Goleman, D. (1995). *Emotional intelligence.* New York: Bantam Books.

Gresham, F. M. (1986). Conceptual and definitional issues in the assessment of children's social skills: Implications for classification and training. *Journal of Clinical Child Psychology, 15*(1), 3–15.

Gresham, F. M., & Elliott, S. (1990). *The Social Skills Rating System.* Circle Pines, MN: American Guidance Service.

Hall, R. V., & Hall, M. C. (1998a). *How to use systematic attention and approval* (2nd ed.). Austin, TX: PRO-ED.

Hall, R. V., & Hall, M. C. (1998b) *How to use time out* (2nd ed.). Austin, TX: PRO-ED.

Hall, R. V., & Van Houten, R. (1977). *Managing behavior: Part 1, Measurement of behavior.* Austin, TX: PRO-ED.

Howell, K. W., & Caros, J. S. (1992). The application of curriculum-based evaluation to social skills. *Diagnostique, 18*(1), 53–68.

Jackson, J. F., Jackson, D. A., & Monroe, C. (1983). *Getting along with others: Teaching social effectiveness to children.* Champaign, IL: Research Press.

Johnson, D. W., Johnson, R. T., & Holubec, E. J. (1994). *Cooperative learning in the classroom.* Alexandria, VA: Association for Supervision and Curriculum Development.

Kratochwill, T. R., & French, D. C. (1984). Social skills training for withdrawn children. *School Psychology Review, 13,* 331–337.

Lewis, T. J. (1994). A comparative analysis of the effects of social skill training and teacher-directed contingencies on social behavior of preschool children with disabilities. *Journal of Behavioral Education, 4*(3), 267–281.

Lewis, T. J. (1996). Functional assessment of problem behavior: A pilot investigation of the comparative and interactive effects of teacher and peer social attention on students in general education settings. *School Psychology Quarterly, 11*(1), 1–19.

Mannix, D. (1986). *I can behave.* Austin, TX: PRO-ED.

Mannix, D. (1995). *Life skills activities for secondary students with special needs.* West Nyack, NY: The Center for Applied Research in Education.

McConnell, S. R. (1987). Entrapment effects and the generalization and maintenance of social skills training for elementary school students with behavioral disorders. *Behavioral Disorders, 12,* 252–263.

McGinnis, E., & Goldstein, A. P. (1984). *Skillstreaming the elementary school child: A guide for teaching prosocial skills.* Champaign, IL: Research Press.

McGinnis, E., & Goldstein, A. P. (1990). *Skillstreaming in early childhood.* Champaign, IL: Research Press.

O'Neill, R., Horner, R., Albin, R., Storey, K., & Sprague, J. (1990). *Functional analysis of problem behavior: A practical assessment guide.* Sycamore, IL: Sycamore.

Phillips, E. L., Phillips, E. A., Fixsen, D. L., & Wolf, M. M. (1974). *The teaching–family handbook* (rev. ed.). Lawrence: University of Kansas Printing Service.

Putallaz, M., & Gottman, J. (1982). Conceptualizing social competence in children. In P. Karoly & J. J. Steffan (Eds.), *Improving children's competence: Advances in child behavior analysis and therapy* (Vol. 1, pp. 1–33). Lexington, MA: Lexington Books.

Rhode, G., Jenson, W. R., & Reavis, H. K. (1992). *The tough kid book.* Longmont, CO: Sopris West.

Slavin, R. E. (1991). *Student team learning* (3rd ed.). Washington, DC: National Education Association.

Stephens, T. M. (1979) *Social Behavior Assessment.* Columbus, OH: Cedars Press.

Strain, P. S., Guralnick, M. J., & Walker, H. M. (Eds.) (1986). *Children's social behavior.* Orlando, FL: Academic Press.

Sugai, G., & Fuller, M. (1991). A decision model for social skills curriculum analysis. *Remedial and Special Education, 12,* 33–42.

Sugai, G., & Lewis, T. J. (1996). Preferred and promising practices for social skills instruction. *Focus on Exceptional Children, 29*(4), 1–16.

Thibadeau, S. (1998). *How to use response cost.* Austin, TX: PRO-ED.

Walker, H. M., & McConnell, S. R. (1988). *The Walker–McConnell Scale of Social Competence and School Adjustment: A social skills rating scale for teachers.* Austin, TX: PRO-ED.

Walker, H. M., McConnell, S., Holmes, D., Todis, B., Walker, J., & Golden, N. (1983). *The Walker Social Skills Curriculum: The ACCEPTS program.* Austin, TX: PRO-ED.

Walker, H. M., Todis, B., Holmes, D., & Horton, G. (1988). *Adolescent curriculum for communication and effective social skills: The ACCESS program.* Austin, TX: PRO-ED.

Wells, P. L. (1991). *School social skills: A teaching approach to schoolwide discipline.* Unpublished manuscript.

Notes

Notes

Notes

Notes

Notes